WALKING BASS LINE CONSTRUCTION
C MINOR BLUES

from the *Pathways Towards Greatness* series

by Bob Sinicrope

SHER MUSIC CO.

© 2024 Sher Music Co., P.O. Box 445, Petaluma, CA, 94953 All Rights Reserved.
International Copyright Secured. Made in the U.S.A. No part of this book may be reproduced
in any form without written permission from the publisher.
ISBN –978-1-883217-82-2

TABLE OF CONTENTS

About *Walking Bass Line Construction - C Minor Blues and Pathways Towards Greatness* series ...iii
About the Author iv
Acknowledgements v
Online Hyperlinks Library vi

Chapter 1   Roots - Internalizing Roots 1

Chapter 2   Add the 5th - Internalizing Roots & 5ths 14

Chapter 3   Add the 3rd - Internalizing Root & 3rds 24

Chapter 4   Add the 7th - Internalizing Seventh Chords 32

Chapter 5   One Measure Patterns 37

Chapter 6   More Patterns 46

Chapter 7   Scales 51

Chapter 8   Minor Clichés 63

Chapter 9   Bass Lines in the Style of 66
              Pops Foster and Walter Page 67
              Milt Hinton and Slam Stewart 68
              Jimmie Blanton and Israel Crosby 69
              George Duvivier and Oscar Pettiford 70
              Percy Heath and Sam Jones 71
              Ray Brown and Red Mitchell 72
              Leroy Vinegar and Andy Simpkins 73
              Paul Chambers and Ron Carter 74
              Charlie Haden and Miroslav Vitous 75
              Bass Line from Backing Track 76

ABOUT WALKING BASS LINE CONSTRUCTION - Bb BLUES AND THE PATHWAYS TOWARDS GREATNESS SERIES

Walking Bass Line Construction — C Minor Blues

This book is dedicated to helping bass players at all levels develop walking bass lines with an emphasis on a learn-by-doing approach. Beginners with limited knowledge of how to spell chords and/or who might be new to playing the bass will have an easy pathway to success and be able to quickly function in a group. The backing track options are unique and playing with them will be fun and help you play with a steady pulse. More experienced players will significantly benefit from this thorough approach. The dozens of hyperlinks will offer novel ideas, explanations, enrichment, and inspiration. The final chapter, emulating the styles of some of the greatest walking bass line masters will be of particular interest to advanced players.

Most exercises in this book have a limited range - low E to middle C on the staff. For 4-string traditional tuning electric bass players this means most of the exercises stay within the first 5 frets.

By no means is this method complete, but it is an efficient way to create bass lines without a mastery of playing or theory. Playing these exercises correctly is a start.

The goal is to internalize and integrate these bass lines so you can apply them to other tunes. Strive to understand the underlying concepts of each exercise. Make them part of your musical vocabulary.

As useful as these exercises might be, the best way to learn bass lines is to emulate aspects of masterful bass lines you hear on recordings. Have fun and play with confidence and joy.

This book is part of the **Pathways towards Greatness** series. Other **Walking Bass Line Construction** books in the works include *All the Things You Are, Autumn Leaves, Bb Blues, Bb Rhythm Changes, F Blues, Perdido, Satin Doll, So What, Summertime, Sugar* and *Take the A Train*.

— Bob Sinicrope

ABOUT THE AUTHOR

photo by Jamey Aebersold

Bob Sinicrope is a consummate educator. He founded the Milton Academy Jazz Program in 1974 and directed it for 50 years. Winner of several national and international awards, the program produced many fine professional musicians, most notably Aaron Goldberg and Steve Lehman. His students performed at multiple Jazz Education conferences, twice at the White House, the North Sea, Fribourg, Viennes, and Montreux Jazz Festivals. They have performed for Eric Alexander, Jim Hall, Dave Holland, Abdullah Ibrahim, Elvin Jones, Steven King, Poncho Sanchez, James Taylor, Desmond Tutu, Kenny Werner, and Victor Wooten and Bass Extremes. Bob's other teaching credits include Jamey Aebersold's Summer Jazz Workshops (40 years), JazzWise Summer School (London, 12 years), and Victor Wooten's Berklee Bass Workshops (7 years). Although Bob has a master's degree in math education, his studies at Berklee College and private lessons with Charlie Banacos, Hal Galper, Rufus Reid, Bob Gullotti, and Mick Goodrick greatly helped him transition to becoming a full-time jazz educator.

In 2007, Bob became the inaugural recipient of the *John LaPorta - Jazz Educator of the Year*. He was a Trustee of the Jazz Education Network (JEN) and was JEN's elected President from 2014-2016. In 2010 Bob received the National Youth Development Council award for his service and also received DownBeat magazine's Jazz Education Achievement Award. Bob has authored several published magazine articles and wrote a chapter in South African bassist Johnny Dyani's biography *Mbizo-Johnny Dyani*. His **Pathways Towards Greatness** SmartMusic improvisation books are used in 63 countries and his series of **Walking Bass Line Construction** books are published by Sher Music.

Bob has made his mark internationally over the past six decades with clinics in schools and conferences on six continents. In 1972, Bob was commissioned to compose *A Question of Balance* for Jamaica's National Dance Theater Company. Since 1991 his special connections with South Africa began when Abdullah Ibrahim visited Milton Academy and invited the school's combo to tour South Africa. His Milton Academy student groups have toured South Africa more than a dozen times and Bob has taught and performed there many times without his students including directing a weeklong workshop for over 100 students at Tshwane University in Pretoria. He also spearheaded the delivery of hundreds of thousands of dollars of donated materials and resources and has forged special bonds with many South African township music programs.

A much-in-demand bassist, Bob's credits include performances with Shirley Bassey, Jerry Bergonzi, Randy Brecker, Sara Caswell, John Clayton, Jeff Coffin, Billy Eckstine,

Bill Evans (saxophone), George Garzone, Aaron Goldberg, Tiny Grimes, Abdullah Ibrahim, Papa Jo Jones, Sean Jones, Mississippi Fred McDowell, Babatunde Olatunji, the Boston Pops, Chris Potter, Rufus Reid, Bobby Sanabria, Kenny Werner, Matt Wilson, Victor Wooten, and the Artie Shaw Band.

Bob can be reached by email at: bob.sinicrope@gmail.com
You can visit his website at: www.bobsinicrope.com

ACKNOWLEDGEMENTS

This method represents the current state of my ongoing learning and understanding of how to help students deepen their ability to freely express themselves in the jazz language. I have been very blessed to have learned from Jamey Aebersold, Christopher Azzara, David Baker, Charlie Banacos, Jerry Bergonzi, Steve Bailey, Gary Burton, Jerry Coker, Hal Crook, Hal Galper, Mick Goodrick, Edwin E. Gordon, Bob Gullotti, Dan Haerle, John LaPorta, Harry Pickens, Herb Pomeroy, Rufus Reid, Kenny Werner and Victor Wooten. These wonderful players/teachers/learners have had a powerful impact on me. Being on the staff of the Aebersold Summer Jazz Workshops for over 40 years, and more recently the Victor Wooten Berklee Bass Weekend Workshop, has provided invaluable enrichment and inspiration.

This project has been greatly enhanced by my editors Eric Goode and Brian Casey. Their advice, keen eyes, perseverance, and encouragement were instrumental in getting this project to completion. John Goldsby was also very helpful with his wisdom, reading and editing. My appreciation also goes to Ted Scalzo for suggesting I share my teachings publicly and for his friendship.

A shout-out also goes to the fine musicians and technicians Mike DiLiddo (guitar and recording), Bobby Floyd (Hammond B3), Barry Lit (drums and recording), Austin Nill (recording), Joel Scanlon (mixing), and Ron Zack (piano) who recorded and/or produced the backing tracks. It was a pleasure for me to play bass with them on these tracks.

My heartfelt thanks to Chuck Sher for his encouragement, significant input, patience and long-standing friendship. It is an honor to be published by Sher Music given their ongoing commitment to jazz education.

Finally, and most significantly, my wife Frances Scanlon has been amazingly helpful with her gifted graphic design skills and editing, and more importantly, her love and support throughout. I thank her for her enthusiasm and commitment to me and this project.

ONLINE HYPERLINKS LIBRARY

This QR code will take you to an **online source of hyperlinks** to various sites that will deepen your understanding of some of the musical concepts presented in ***Walking Bass Line Construction – C Minor Blues***.

Each page of exercises has commentary and a title in *underlined* text.

This *underlined* text is an indication that the online source of hyperlinks can help you further your development.

CHAPTER 1

Roots - Internalizing Roots

#1.1

C Minor Blues
Walking Bass Line
Roots - Internalizing Roots

Roots are the foundation of a tune's harmony and the most consonant note in any chord.

Learning to hear the Roots will help you keep your place in the form of the tune.

Sing and play Roots on all tunes to help internalize their sound.

Play with vigor!

To more fully internalize:
1. Listen
2. Sing
3. Play

by Bob Sinicrope

Inspiration, Education, Fun
©2024 SeekingSpirit

#1.2

Approach Notes *are tension notes that resolve to chord tones. They add melodic interest and create rhythmic motion. The resolution is stronger if the approach note is on an upbeat and the chord tone is on a downbeat.*

*This exercise features **Lower Chromatic (LC)** Approach notes to the **Root (R)**. These work well in bass lines.*

Make it dance!

C Minor Blues
Walking Bass Line
Roots - Lower Chromatic to Root

To more fully internalize:
1. Listen
2. Sing
3. Play

by Bob Sinicrope

Inspiration, Education, Fun
©2024 SeekingSpirit

WALKING BASS LINE CONSTRUCTION | C Minor Blues

#1.5

Approach Notes *are tension notes that resolve to chord tones. They add melodic interest and create rhythmic motion. The resolution is stronger if the approach note is on an upbeat and the chord tone is on a downbeat.*

This exercise features Upper Chromatic (UC) *approach notes to the* **Root (R)**. *These do not always work well. Once you learn them, you can choose when you want to use them.*

Play with power!

C Minor Blues Walking Bass Line
Roots - Upper Chromatic to Root

To more fully internalize:
1. Listen
2. Sing
3. Play

by Bob Sinicrope

Inspiration, Education, Fun
©2024 SeekingSpirit

#1.6

C Minor Blues
Walking Bass Line
Roots - Upper Double Chromatic to Root

Approach Notes are tension notes that resolve to chord tones. They add melodic interest and create rhythmic motion. The resolution is stronger if the Approach Note is on an upbeat and the chord tone is on a downbeat.

*This exercise features **Double Chromatic (UD Approach Notes** to the **Root (R)**. These sometimes, but not always work well in bass lines.*

Play with zest!

To more fully internalize:
1. Listen
2. Sing
3. Play

by Bob Sinicrope

#1.7

Approach Notes *are tension notes that resolve to chord tones. They add melodic interest and create rhythmic motion. The resolution is stronger if the Approach Note is on an upbeat and the chord tone is on a downbeat.*

This exercise features **Upper Triple Chromatic (UTC)** *approach notes to the* **Root (R)**. *These do not always work well. Once you learn them, you can choose when you want to use them.*

Make your notes ring out!

C Minor Blues Walking Bass Line
Roots - Upper Triple Chromatic to Root

To more fully internalize:
1. *Listen*
2. *Sing*
3. *Play*

by Bob Sinicrope

Inspiration, Education, Fun
©2024 SeekingSpirit

#1.8

C Minor Blues
Walking Bass Line
Roots - Upper Scalar to Root

To more fully internalize:
1. Listen
2. Sing
3. Play

Approach Notes *are tension notes that resolve to chord tones. They add melodic interest and create rhythmic motion. The resolution is stronger if the approach note is on an upbeat and the chord tone is on a downbeat.*

*This exercise features an **Upper Scalar** (US) Approach Note to the **Root (R)**.*

Make your notes powerful!

by Bob Sinicrope

Inspiration, Education, Fun
©2024 SeekingSpirit

WALKING BASS LINE CONSTRUCTION | C Minor Blues

#1.11

Enclosures combine Lower and Upper Approach Notes that resolve to chord tones. They add melodic interest and create rhythmic motion.

This exercise features Lower Double Chromatics (LD) and Upper Scalar (US) approach notes.

It also has Forward Motion where the Approach Notes resolve to a chord tone on a strong downbeat.

Play with expression!

C Minor Blues
Walking Bass Line

Roots - Enclosure #3
Lower Double Chromatic - Upper Scalar to Root
Upper Scalar - Lower Double Chromatic to Root

by Bob Sinicrope

To more fully internalize:
1. Listen
2. Sing
3. Play

WALKING BASS LINE CONSTRUCTION | C Minor Blues

#1.12

This exercise incorporates the concepts presented in this chapter. Have fun creating your own bass lines that use Roots, Octaves, Lower Chromatics, Lower Double Chromatics, Triple Lower Chromatics Upper Chromatics, Upper Double Chromatics, Upper Triple Chromatics, and Upper Scalars and Enclosures.

Play what you love; love what you play!

C Minor Blues
Walking Bass Line
Roots - Summary

To more fully internalize:
1. Listen
2. Sing
3. Play

by Bob Sinicrope

Inspiration, Education, Fun
©2024 SeekingSpirit

WALKING BASS LINE CONSTRUCTION | C Minor Blues

CHAPTER 2

Add the 5th - Internalizing Roots & 5ths

#2.1

Bassists frequently utilize **Roots**, **5ths** and **Octaves** in their bass lines. These make a strong harmonic foundation. It's important to become comfortable with these patterns.

Sing and play **Roots (R)**, **5ths (5)** and **Octaves (R̂)** on all tunes to help internalize their sound.

Play with energy!

C Minor Blues Walking Bass Line
Add the 5th - Internalizing Roots & 5ths

To more fully internalize:
1. Listen
2. Sing
3. Play

by Bob Sinicrope

Inspiration, Education, Fun
©2024 SeekingSpirit

WALKING BASS LINE CONSTRUCTION | C Minor Blues

#2.2

Bassists frequently utilize **Roots, 5ths and Octaves** in their bass lines. These make a strong harmonic foundation. It's important to become comfortable with these patterns.

Sing and play **Roots (R), 5ths (5) and Octaves (R̂)** on all tunes to help internalize their sound.

Play with a ping and a ring!

C Minor Blues Walking Bass Line
Add the 5th - Internalizing Roots, 5ths and Octaves #1

To more fully internalize:
1. Listen
2. Sing
3. Play

by Bob Sinicrope

WALKING BASS LINE CONSTRUCTION | C Minor Blues

Inspiration, Education, Fun
©2024 SeekingSpirit

#2.3

*Bassists frequently utilize **Roots**, **5ths** and **Octaves** in their bass lines. These make a strong harmonic foundation. It's important to become comfortable with these patterns.*

*Sing and play **Roots**, **5ths** and **Octaves** on all tunes to help internalize their sound.*

Play with confidence!

C Minor Blues
Walking Bass Line
Add the 5th - Internalizing Roots, 5ths and Octaves #2

To more fully internalize:
1. Listen
2. Sing
3. Play

by Bob Sinicrope

Inspiration, Education, Fun
©2024 SeekingSpirit

WALKING BASS LINE CONSTRUCTION | C Minor Blues

#2.4

C Minor Blues Walking Bass Line
Add the 5th - Lower Chromatic to Root

Approach Notes are tension notes that resolve to chord tones. They add melodic interest and create rhythmic motion. The resolution is stronger if the approach note is on an upbeat and the chord tone is on a downbeat.

This exercise features **Lower Chromatic** (**LC**) *Approach Notes to the* **Root** (**R** *or* **R̂**). *These work well in bass lines.*

Make it feel great!

To more fully internalize:
1. Listen
2. Sing
3. Play

by Bob Sinicrope

Inspiration. Education. Fun
©2024 SeekingSpirit

#2.5

C Minor Blues
Walking Bass Line
Add the 5th - Upper Scalar to Root

To more fully internalize:
1. Listen
2. Sing
3. Play

Approach Notes *are tension notes that resolve to chord tones. They add melodic interest and create rhythmic motion. The resolution is stronger if the approach note is on an upbeat and the chord tone is on a downbeat.*

This exercise features **Upper Scalar (US)** *Approach Notes to the* **Root (R)** *and* **Octave (R̂)**.

Feel the pulse!

by Bob Sinicrope

Inspiration, Education, Fun
©2024 SeekingSpirit

WALKING BASS LINE CONSTRUCTION | C Minor Blues

#2.6

Approach Notes are tension notes that resolve to chord tones. They add melodic interest and create rhythmic motion. The resolution is stronger if the approach note is on an upbeat and the chord tone is on a downbeat.

*This exercise features **Lower Chromatic (LC)** Approach Notes to the **5th (5)**. These work well in bass lines.*

Play with a beautiful sound!

C Minor Blues Walking Bass Line
Add the 5th - Lower Chromatic to 5th

To more fully internalize:
1. Listen
2. Sing
3. Play

by Bob Sinicrope

Inspiration, Education, Fun
©2024 SeekingSpirit

WALKING BASS LINE CONSTRUCTION | C Minor Blues

#2.7

Approach Notes *are tension notes that resolve to chord tones. They add melodic interest and create rhythmic motion. The resolution is stronger if the approach note is on an upbeat and the chord tone is on a downbeat.*

This exercise features **Upper Scalar (US)** *Approach Notes to the* **5th (5)**. *These work well in bass lines.*

Connect with the backing track!

C Minor Blues Walking Bass Line
Add the 5th - Upper Scalar to 5th

To more fully internalize:
1. Listen
2. Sing
3. Play

by Bob Sinicrope

#2.8

Enclosures combine Lower and Upper Approach Notes *that resolve to chord tones. They add melodic interest and create rhythmic motion.*

*This exercise features **Lower Chromatic (LC)** and **Upper Scalar (US)** Approach Notes to the 5th.*

Focus on what you play!

C Minor Blues Walking Bass Line
Add the 5th - Enclosure

To more fully internalize:
1. Listen
2. Sing
3. Play

by Bob Sinicrope

22   WALKING BASS LINE CONSTRUCTION | C Minor Blues

CHAPTER 3

Add the 3rd - Internalizing Root & 3rds

#3.1

Roots (R), Octaves (R̂) & 3rds (3) are the chord tones. The 3rd is a Defining Tone that determines if the triad is major or minor. Strong bass lines imply the harmony and defining tones strongly suggest the harmony.

Experiment creating your own bass lines with Roots, Octaves and 3rds.

Play with positivity!

C Minor Blues
Walking Bass Line
Add the 3rd - Internalizing Root & 3rds

To more fully internalize:
1. Listen
2. Sing
3. Play

by Bob Sinicrope

Inspiration, Education, Fun
©2024 SeekingSpirit

WALKING BASS LINE CONSTRUCTION | C Minor Blues

#3.3

C Minor Blues Walking Bass Line
Add the 3rd - Lower Chromatic to the 3rd

Approach Notes are tension notes that resolve to chord tones. They add melodic interest and create rhythmic motion.

This exercise features Lower Chromatic (LC) Approach Notes to the 3rd (3). These work well in bass lines.

Be the heartbeat!

To more fully internalize:
1. Listen
2. Sing
3. Play

by Bob Sinicrope

Inspiration, Education, Fun
©2024 SeekingSpirit

WALKING BASS LINE CONSTRUCTION | C Minor Blues

#3.4

Approach Notes are tension notes that resolve to chord tones. They add melodic interest and create rhythmic motion.

This exercise features **Upper Scalar (US)** Approach Notes to the **3rd (3)**. They add flavor to your bass line.

Play every note as if it's the most important note you'll ever play!

C Minor Blues Walking Bass Line
Add the 3rd - Upper Scalar to the 3rd

To more fully internalize:
1. Listen
2. Sing
3. Play

by Bob Sinicrope

Inspiration, Education, Fun
©2024 SeekingSpirit

#3.6

Enclosures combine Lower and Upper Approach Notes *that resolve to chord tones. They add melodic interest and create rhythmic motion. Although not the strongest bass line figure, it is a valid option.*

This exercise features **Lower Chromatic (LC) and Upper Scalar (US)** *Approach Notes.*

Mean what you play!

C Minor Blues
Walking Bass Line
Add the 3rd - Enclosure to the 3rd

To more fully internalize:
1. Listen
2. Sing
3. Play

by Bob Sinicrope

Inspiration, Education, Fun
©2024 SeekingSpirit

WALKING BASS LINE CONSTRUCTION | C Minor Blues

#3.7

This exercise incorporates the concepts presented in this chapter. Have fun creating your own bass lines that use Roots, 3rds, Octaves, Lower Chromatics, Upper Scalars and Enclosures.

Have a positive attitude!

C Minor Blues
Walking Bass Line
Add the 3rd - Summary

To more fully internalize:
1. Listen
2. Sing
3. Play

by Bob Sinicrope

Inspiration, Education, Fun
©2024 SeekingSpirit

WALKING BASS LINE CONSTRUCTION | C Minor Blues

CHAPTER 4

Add the 7th - Internalizing Seventh Chords

#4.2

These patterns work well with a shuffle feel.

Experiment with your own bass lines with Roots (R), 5ths (5), 7ths (7) and Octaves (R̂).

Emulate all aspects of a masterful bass player!

C Minor Blues
Walking Bass Line
Add the 7th - Patterns #1

To more fully internalize:
1. Listen
2. Sing
3. Play

by Bob Sinicrope

Inspiration, Education, Fun
©2024 SeekingSpirit

#4.3

These patterns work well with a shuffle feel.

Experiment with your own bass lines with Roots (R), 7ths (7) and Octaves (R̂).

Be the pulse!

C Minor Blues
Walking Bass Line
Add the 7th - Patterns #2

To more fully internalize:
1. Listen
2. Sing
3. Play

by Bob Sinicrope

#4.4

This exercise incorporates the concepts presented in this chapter. Have fun creating your own bass lines that use Roots, 3rds, 5ths, 7th, Octaves, and Patterns.

Be consistent!

C Minor Blues Walking Bass Line
Add the 7th - Summary

To more fully internalize:
1. Listen
2. Sing
3. Play

by Bob Sinicrope

WALKING BASS LINE CONSTRUCTION | C Minor Blues

CHAPTER 5

One Measure Patterns

#5.1

C Minor Blues
Walking Bass Line
One Measure Patterns - R235 532R

To more fully internalize:
1. Listen
2. Sing
3. Play

A Passing Tone is a note between chord tones that connects them. The chord tones are consonant notes and the passing tone creates tension that resolves. Musical "tension and release" is an important concept that adds interest and motion to your playing.

Passing Tones make for strong bass lines.

Make it Groove!

by Bob Sinicrope

Inspiration, Education, Fun
©2024 SeekingSpirit

WALKING BASS LINE CONSTRUCTION | C Minor Blues

#5.2

C Minor Blues
Walking Bass Line
One Measure Patterns - R345 543R

A Passing Tone is a note between chord tones that connects them. The chord tones are consonant notes and the passing tone creates tension that resolves. Musical "tension and release" is an important concept that adds interest and motion to your playing.

Passing Tones make for strong bass lines.

Drive the Band!

To more fully internalize:
1. Listen
2. Sing
3. Play

by Bob Sinicrope

Inspiration, Education, Fun
©2024 SeekingSpirit

#5.3

A Passing Tone is a note between chord tones that connects them. The chord tones are consonant notes and the passing tone creates tension that resolves. Musical "tension and release" is an important concept that adds interest and motion to your playing.

Passing Tones make for strong bass lines.

Go for flow!

C Minor Blues
Walking Bass Line
One Measure Patterns - R̂345 543R̂

To more fully internalize:
1. Listen
2. Sing
3. Play

by Bob Sinicrope

WALKING BASS LINE CONSTRUCTION | C Minor Blues

Inspiration, Education, Fun
©2024 SeekingSpirit

#5.4

C Minor Blues Walking Bass Line
One Measure Patterns - R365-R̂653

*This bass line uses a one measure pattern using the **Root (R), 3rd (3), 6th (6), 5th (5), and Octaves (R̂)**.*

Experiment with using 6 and b6. Each offers a different 'flavor' to your bass line. Use your ears as which one to use and when.

Sing through your bass!

To more fully internalize:
1. Listen
2. Sing
3. Play

by Bob Sinicrope

Inspiration, Education, Fun
©2024 SeekingSpirit

#5.7

C Minor Blues
Walking Bass Line
One Measure Patterns - R̂765-R̂7(LC)5

*These bass lines feature **Octaves (R̂), 7ths (7), 6ths (6), 5ths (5)** and **Lower Chromatic (LC)** patterns.*

Experiment with using 6 and b6. Each offers a different 'flavor' to your bass line. Use your ears as which one to use and when.

Play as if no one can hear you!

To more fully internalize:
1. Listen
2. Sing
3. Play

by Bob Sinicrope

Inspiration, Education, Fun
©2024 SeekingSpirit

#5.8

This exercise incorporates the concepts presented in this chapter. Have fun creating your own bass lines that use One Measure Patterns.

Strive for effortless mastery!

C Minor Blues
Walking Bass Line
One Measure Patterns - Summary

To more fully internalize:
1. Listen
2. Sing
3. Play

by Bob Sinicrope

Inspiration, Education, Fun
©2024 SeekingSpirit

WALKING BASS LINE CONSTRUCTION | C Minor Blues

CHAPTER 6

More Patterns

#6.1

This bass lines feature two measure patterns with slight variations.

Play from your heart!

C Minor Blues
Walking Bass Line
More Patterns - #1

To more fully internalize:
1. Listen
2. Sing
3. Play

by Bob Sinicrope

* Backing Track may not harmonically agree with the scale pitches.

Inspiration, Education, Fun
©2024 SeekingSpirit

#6.2

This bass lines feature two measure patterns with slight variations.

Experiment with adding 6 and b6. Each offers a different 'flavor' to your bass line. Use your ears to determine which one to use and when.

Be in the Moment!

C Minor Blues
Walking Bass Line
More Patterns - #2

To more fully internalize:
1. *Listen*
2. *Sing*
3. *Play*

by Bob Sinicrope

Inspiration, Education, Fun
©2024 SeekingSpirit

#6.3

This bass line features two measure patterns.

Experiment with using 6 and b6 and b7 and 7. Each offers a different 'flavor' to your bass line. Use your ears to determine which one to use and when.

Learn to play less and you will say more!

C Minor Blues
Walking Bass Line
More Patterns - #3

To more fully internalize:
1. Listen
2. Sing
3. Play

by Bob Sinicrope

#6.4

This bass line features two measure patterns.

*Experiment with using **6** and **b6** and **b7** and **7**. Each offers a different 'flavor' to your bass line. Use your ears to determine which one to use and when.*

Don't play the bass, let it play you!

C Minor Blues
Walking Bass Line
More Patterns - Summary

To more fully internalize:
1. Listen
2. Sing
3. Play

by Bob Sinicrope

* Backing Track may not harmonically agree with the scale pitches.

WALKING BASS LINE CONSTRUCTION | C Minor Blues

CHAPTER 7

Scales

#7.2

C Minor Blues
Walking Bass Line
Scales - Aeolian Minor Scale

*This bass line features the **Aeolian Minor Scale** also called the **Pure Minor or Natural Minor Scale**. It is constructed by making the 3rd, 6th and 7th of a major scale flat resulting in R 2 b3 4 5 b6 b7 R̂. Playing the notes from a Major Scale but starting and ending on the 6th degree of that Major Scale will also result in an Aeolian Minor Scale.*

Music is the space between the notes!

To more fully internalize:
1. Listen
2. Sing
3. Play

by Bob Sinicrope

Inspiration, Education, Fun
©2024 SeekingSpirit

#7.3

*This bass line features the **Harmonic Minor Scale**. It is constructed by making the 3rd and 6th of a major scale flat resulting in **R 2 b3 4 5 b6 7 R̂**.*

Strive to play what you hear, not hear what you play!

C Minor Blues
Walking Bass Line

Scales - Harmonic Minor Scale

To more fully internalize:
1. Listen
2. Sing
3. Play

by Bob Sinicrope

Inspiration, Education, Fun
©2024 SeekingSpirit

WALKING BASS LINE CONSTRUCTION | C Minor Blues

#7.4

C Minor Blues Walking Bass Line

Scales - Melodic Minor (Jazz Minor) Scale

*This bass line features the **Melodic Minor Scale**. It is also called the **Jazz Minor Scale**. When ascending, the scale is constructed by making the 3rd of a major scale flat resulting in **R 2 b3 4 5 6 7 R̂**. When descending, the scale reverts to Aeolian Minor **R̂ b7 b6 5 4 b3 2 R**. When descending, you could also explore playing **R̂ 7 6 5 4 b3 2 R**. Experiment.*

Be supportive and encouraging of your bandmates!

To more fully internalize:
1. Listen
2. Sing
3. Play

by Bob Sinicrope

Inspiration, Education, Fun
©2024 SeekingSpirit

WALKING BASS LINE CONSTRUCTION | C Minor Blues   55

#7.5

This bass line features a comparison of the different minor scales. Notice the differences between the b6 and 6 and b7 and 7. Each scale offers a different 'flavor' to your bass line. Use your ears to determine which one to use and when to use it.

It's not what you play, it's how you play it!

C Minor Blues
Walking Bass Line
Minor Scales Comparison

To more fully internalize:
1. Listen
2. Sing
3. Play

by Bob Sinicrope

Inspiration. Education. Fun
©2024 SeekingSpirit

#7.6

These bass lines feature the Bebop Scale. The Bebop Scale has an additional note (italicized underlined text) inserted with the goal of placing important chord tones on the stronger downbeats of 1 and 3 (bold text). This contributes to a better flow of the bass line while emphasizing the "flavor" of the scale. The Bebop Scale is very effective for soloing with 8th note rhythms. Although it can be used ascending or descending it's a little stronger descending. Play with purpose!

C Minor Blues Walking Bass Line

Scales - Bebop Scale Bass Lines #1&2

To more fully internalize:
1. Listen
2. Sing
3. Play

Swing 8ths   * Backing Track may not harmonically agree with the scale pitches.

by Bob Sinicrope

Inspiration, Education, Fun
©2024 SeekingSpirit

WALKING BASS LINE CONSTRUCTION | C Minor Blues

#7.7

These bass lines feature the Bebop Scale. The Bebop Scale has an additional note (italicized underlined text) inserted with the goal of placing important chord tone on the stronger downbeats of 1 and 3 (bold text). This contributes to a better flow of the bass line while emphasizing the "flavor" of the scale. The Bebop Scale is very effective for soloing with 8th note rhythms. Although it can be used ascending or descending it's a little stronger descending.

Music is life - that's why our hearts have beats!

C Minor Blues Walking Bass Line

Scales - Bebop Scale Bass Lines #3&4

To more fully internalize:
1. Listen
2. Sing
3. Play

Swing 8ths * Backing Track may not harmonically agree with the scale pitches.

by Bob Sinicrope

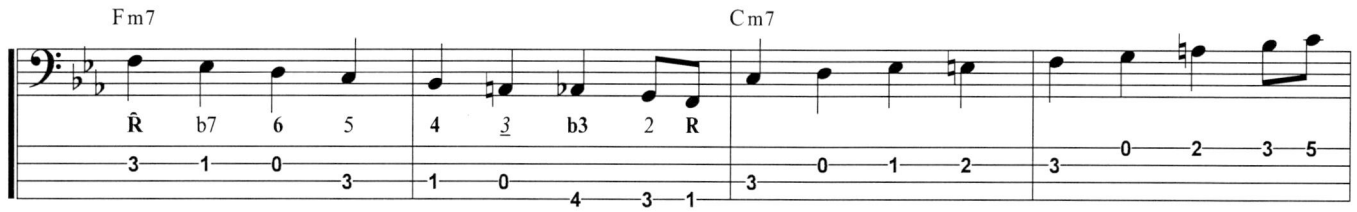

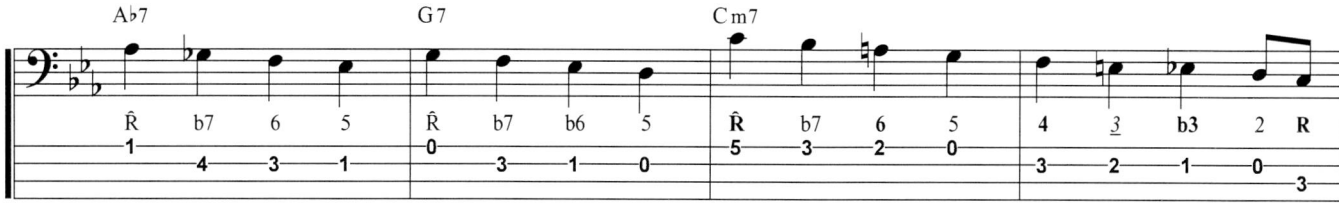

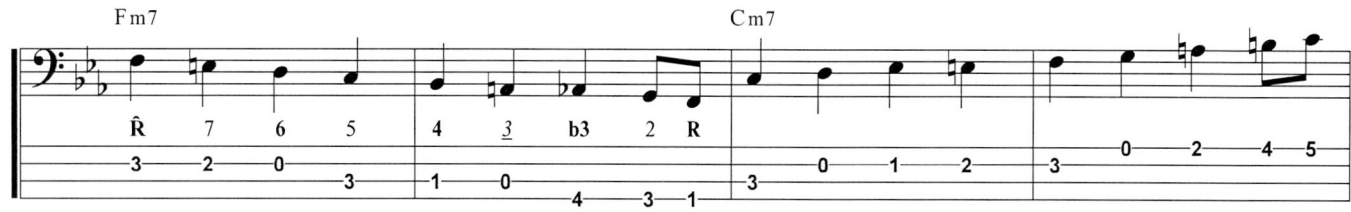

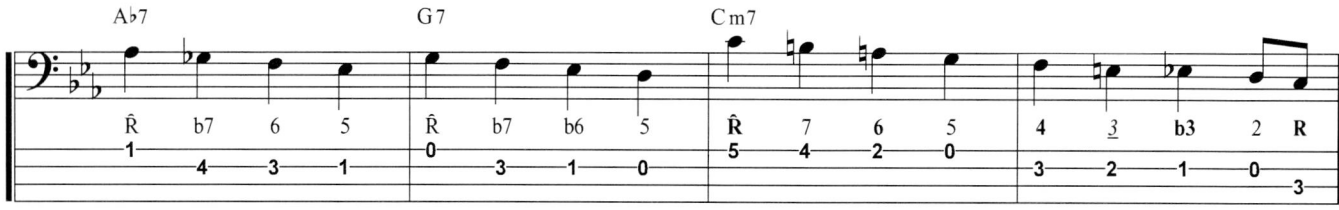

Inspiration, Education, Fun
©2024 SeekingSpirit

#7.8

These bass lines feature the Bebop Scale. The Bebop Scale has an additional note (italicized underlined text) inserted with the goal of placing important chord tone on the stronger downbeats of 1 and 3 (bold text). This contributes to a better flow of the bass line while emphasizing the "flavor" of the scale. The Bebop Scale is very effective for soloing with 8th note rhythms. Although it can be used ascending or descending it's a little stronger descending.

Be patient with yourself and others!

C Minor Blues Walking Bass Line
Scales - Bebop Scale Bass Lines #5&6

To more fully internalize:
1. Listen
2. Sing
3. Play

by Bob Sinicrope

Inspiration, Education, Fun
©2024 SeekingSpirit

WALKING BASS LINE CONSTRUCTION | C Minor Blues

#7.9

*These bass lines feature the Bebop Scale. The Bebop Scale has an additional note (italicized underlined text) inserted with the goal of placing important chord tone on the stronger downbeats of **1** and **3** (bold text). This contributes to a better flow of the bass line while emphasizing the "flavor" of the scale. The Bebop Scale is very effective for soloing with 8th note rhythms. Although it can be used ascending or descending it's a little stronger descending.*

The expert at anything was once a beginer!

C Minor Blues
Walking Bass Line
Scales - Bebop Scale Bass Lines #7&8

To more fully internalize:
1. Listen
2. Sing
3. Play

Swing 8ths   * Backing Track may not harmonically agree with the scale pitches.

by Bob Sinicrope

Inspiration, Education, Fun
©2024 SeekingSpirit

WALKING BASS LINE CONSTRUCTION | C Minor Blues

#7.10

These bass lines feature the Bebop Scale. The Bebop Scale has an additional note (italicized underlined text) inserted with the goal of placing important chord tone on the stronger downbeats of 1 and 3 (bold text). This contributes to a better flow of the bass line while emphasizing the "flavor" of the scale. The Bebop Scale is very effective for soloing with 8th note rhythms. Although it can be used ascending or descending it's a little stronger descending.

Develop your musical personality!

C Minor Blues
Walking Bass Line
Scales - Bebop Scale Bass Lines #9&10

To more fully internalize:
1. Listen
2. Sing
3. Play

by Bob Sinicrope

Swing 8ths   * Backing Track may not harmonically agree with the scale pitches.

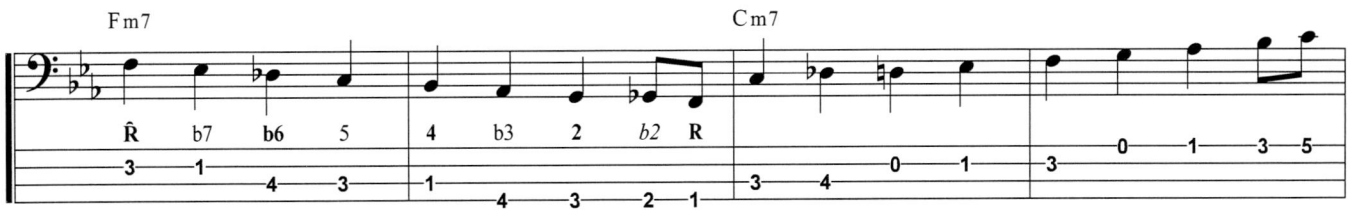
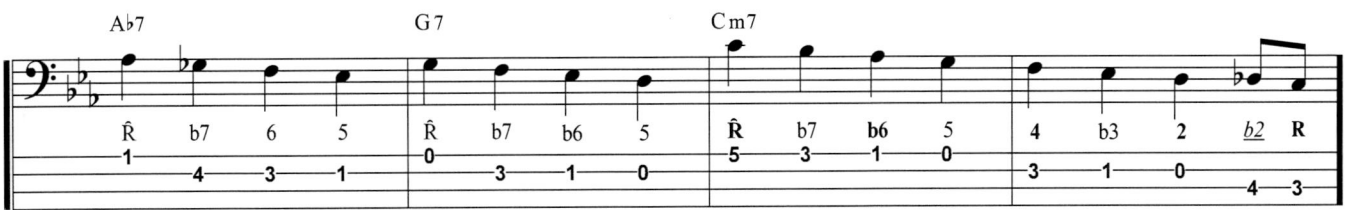
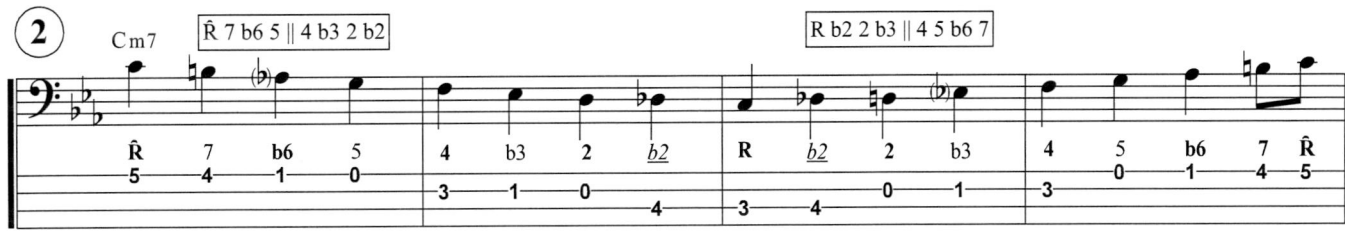
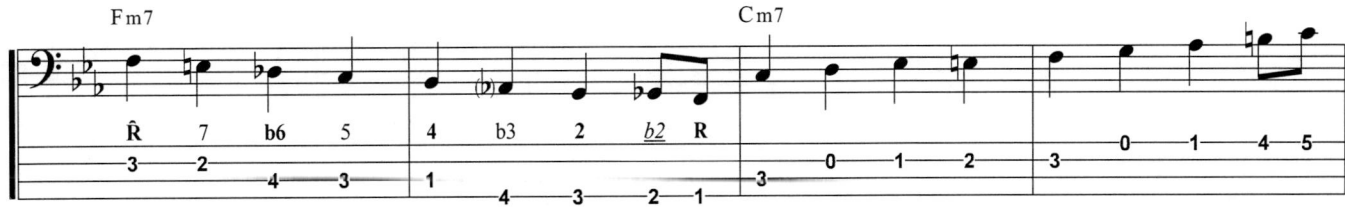
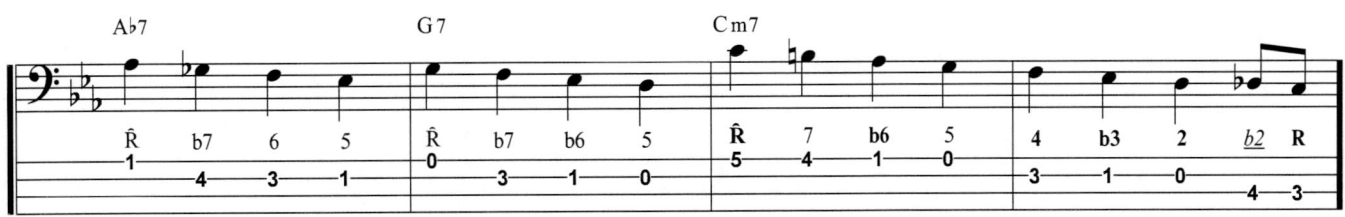

Inspiration, Education, Fun
©2024 SeekingSpirit

WALKING BASS LINE CONSTRUCTION | C Minor Blues

CHAPTER 8

Minor Clichés

#8.1

C Minor Blues Walking Bass Line
Line Cliché - Minor Descending from the Root

by Bob Sinicrope

*This exercise features several versions of a **descending minor line cliché**. It involves 1/2 steps descending from the root. It works very well with minor chords that last 4 measures but can be used for fewer measures.*

***Blue Skies, I Just Called to Say I Love You, In a Sentimental Mood, Michelle, My Funny Valentine,** and **Afro-Cuban ostinatos** are great examples of tunes that feature this approach.*

Music is the soundtrack of your life!

To more fully internalize:
1. Listen
2. Sing
3. Play

WALKING BASS LINE CONSTRUCTION | C Minor Blues

#8.2

*This exercise features several versions of an **ascending minor line cliché from the 5th**. It involves 1/2 steps ascending and descending from the fifth. It works very well with minor chords that last 4 measures but can be used for fewer measures.*

For Once in My Life, Goldfinger and The Greatest Love of All are great examples of tunes that feature this approach.

Let your music change the world!

C Minor Blues
Walking Bass Line
Line Cliché - Minor Ascending from the 5th

by Bob Sinicrope

To more fully internalize:
1. Listen
2. Sing
3. Play

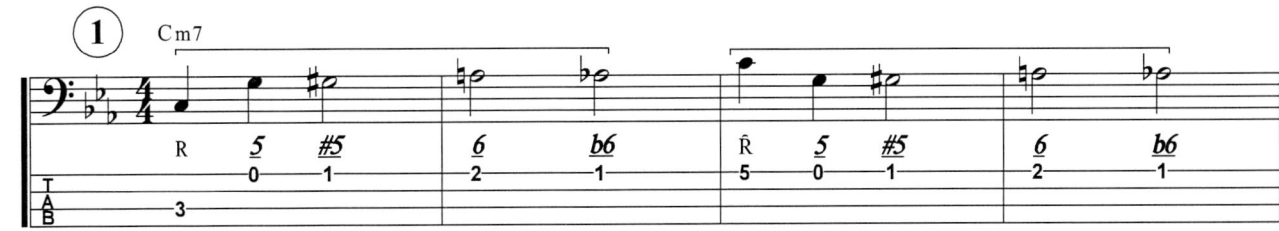

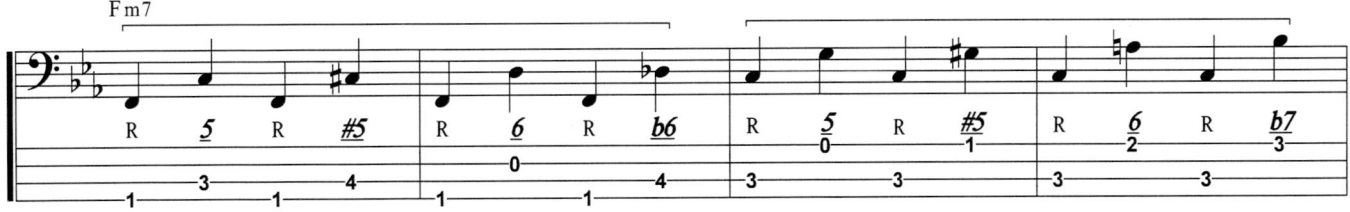

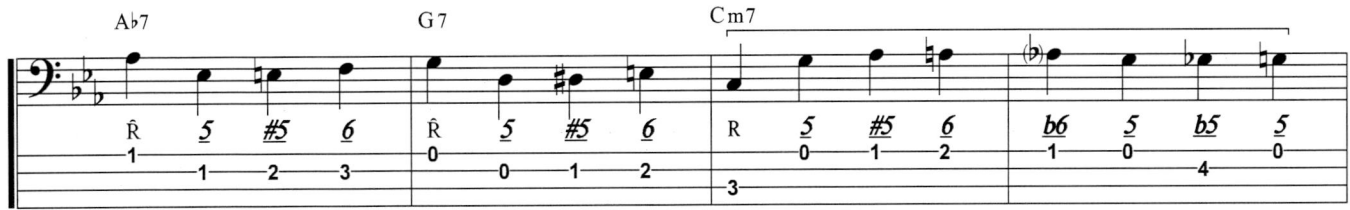

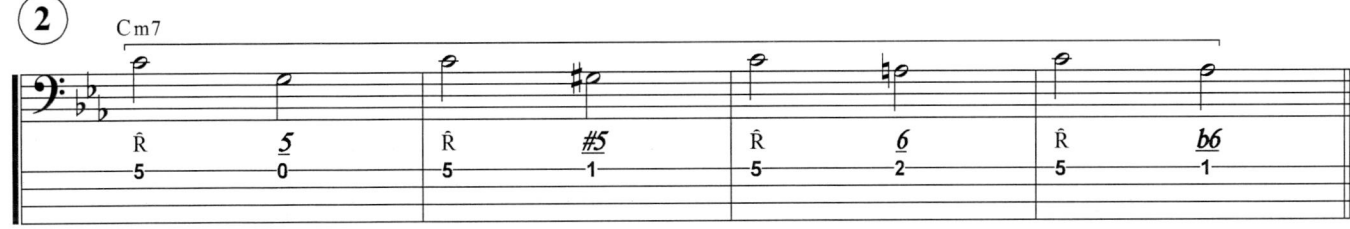

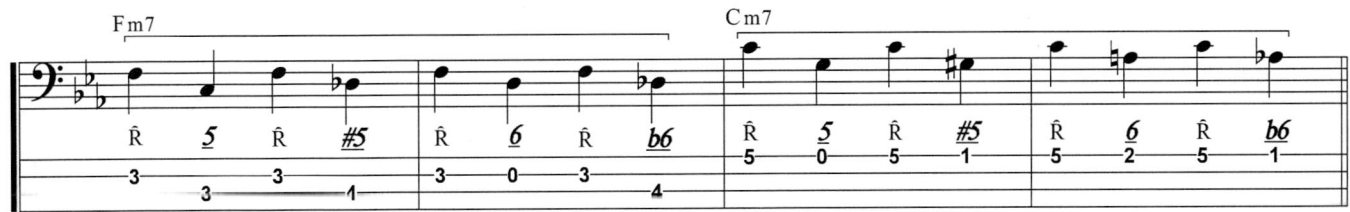

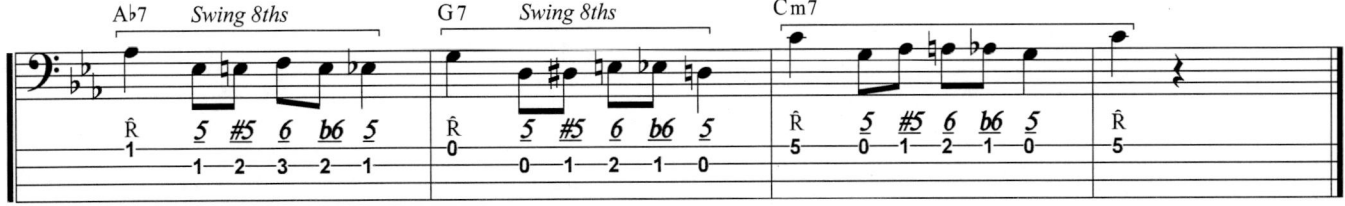

Inspiration, Education, Fun
©2024 SeekingSpirit

WALKING BASS LINE CONSTRUCTION | C Minor Blues

CHAPTER 9

Bass Lines in the style of . . . .

Pops Foster and Walter Page
Milt Hinton and Slam Stewart
Jimmie Blanton and Israel Crosby
George Duvivier and Oscar Pettiford
Percy Heath and Sam Jones
Ray Brown and Red Mitchell
Leroy Vinegar and Andy Simpkins
Paul Chambers and Ron Carter
Charlie Haden and Miroslav Vitous
Bass Line from Backing Track

#9.1

These bass lines mimic the style of two pioneers of Jazz Bass playing, Pops Foster and Walter Page.

Learn about some awesome walking jazz bass players.

C Minor Blues
Walking Bass Line

Bass Lines in the style of
1. Pops Foster and 2. Walter Page

To more fully internalize:
1. Listen
2. Sing
3. Play

WALKING BASS LINE CONSTRUCTION | C Minor Blues

#9.3

These bass lines mimic the style of Jimmie Blanton and Israel Crosby.

Learn about some awesome walking jazz bass players.

C Minor Blues
Walking Bass Line
Bass Lines in the style of
1. Jimmie Blanton and 2. Israel Crosby

To more fully internalize:
1. Listen
2. Sing
3. Play

by Bob Sinicrope

Inspiration, Education, Fun
©2024 SeekingSpirit

WALKING BASS LINE CONSTRUCTION | C Minor Blues

#9.4

These bass lines mimic the style of George Duvivier and Oscar Pettiford.

Learn about some awesome walking jazz bass players.

C Minor Blues
Walking Bass Line
Bass Lines in the style of
1. George Duvivier and 2. Oscar Pettiford

To more fully internalize:
1. Listen
2. Sing
3. Play

Inspiration, Education, Fun
©2024 SeekingSpirit

WALKING BASS LINE CONSTRUCTION | C Minor Blues

#9.5

This bass line mimics the style of Percy Heath and Sam Jones.

Learn about some awesome walking jazz bass players.

C Minor Blues
Walking Bass Line
Bass Lines in the style of
1. Percy Heath 2. Sam Jones

To more fully internalize:
1. Listen
2. Sing
3. Play

by Bob Sinicrope

Inspiration, Education, Fun
©2024 SeekingSpirit

WALKING BASS LINE CONSTRUCTION | C Minor Blues

#9.6

These bass lines mimic the style of bassist Ray Brown and Red Mitchell.

Learn about some awesome walking jazz bass players.

C Minor Blues
Walking Bass Line

Bass Lines in the style of
1. Ray Brown and 2. Red Mitchell

To more fully internalize:
1. Listen
2. Sing
3. Play

by Bob Sinicrope

Inspiration, Education, Fun
©2024 SeekingSpirit

WALKING BASS LINE CONSTRUCTION | C Minor Blues

#9.9

These bass lines mimic the style of Charlie Haden and Miroslav Vitous.

Learn about some awesome walking jazz bass players.

C Minor Blues
Walking Bass Line
Bass Lines in the style of
1. Charlie Haden 2. Miroslav Vitous

To more fully internalize:
1. Listen
2. Sing
3. Play

Inspiration, Education, Fun
©2024 SeekingSpirit

WALKING BASS LINE CONSTRUCTION | C Minor Blues

The Sher Music Co. Catalog
visit **SherMusic.com** for more information and to order online.

BEST-SELLING BOOKS BY MARK LEVINE
The Jazz Theory Book
The Jazz Piano Book
Jazz Piano Masterclass: The Drop 2 Book
How To Voice Standards at the Piano

THE WORLD'S BEST FAKE BOOKS
The New Real Book - Vol. 1 - C, Bb and Eb
The New Real Book - Vol. 2 - C, Bb and Eb
The New Real Book - Vol. 3 - C, Bb, Eb & Bass Clef

The Real Easy Book - Vol. 1 - C, Bb, Eb & Bass Clef
The Real Easy Book - Vol. 2 - C, Bb, Eb & Bass Clef
The Real Easy Book - Vol. 3 - C, Bb, Eb & Bass Clef
The Latin Real Easy Book - C, Bb, Eb & Bass Clef
Drum Supplement for Real Easy Book - Vol. 1

The Standards Real Book - C, Bb and Eb
The Latin Real Book - C, Bb and Eb
The Real Cool Book - Octet charts from the 1950s
The All-Jazz Real Book - with selected audio
The European Real Book - with selected audio
The Best of Sher Music Real Books - C, Bb & Eb
The World's Greatest Fake Book - C only
Jazz Arrangements of Public Domain Songs
The Yellowjackets Songbook - separate parts

LATIN MUSIC BOOKS
Contemporary Latin Jazz Guitar - by Neff Irizarry
Decoding Afro-Cuban Jazz - by Mauleon & Valdes
The Salsa Guidebook - by Rebeca Mauleōn
101 Montunos - by Rebeca Mauleōn
The Latin Bass Book - by Oscar Stagnaro & Chuck Sher
The Latin Real Book - C, Bb, & Eb
The True Cuban Bass - by Carlos del Puerto
The Brazilian Guitar Book - by Nelson Faria
Inside the Brazilian Rhythm Section - Faria/Korman
Conga Drummer's Guidebook - by Michael Spiro
Language of the Masters - by Michael Spiro
Introduction to the Conga Drum DVD - by M. Spiro
Afro-Caribbean Grooves for Drumset - JPhi Fanfant
Afro-Peruvian Percussion Ensemble - H. Morales
Flamenco Improvisation - Vol.1-3 by Enrique Vargas
Muy Caliente! - Afro-Cuban Book & Play-Aong audio
Music of the Arará Savalú Cabildo - Galvin & Spiro

DIGITAL FAKE BOOKS
The New Real Book - Vol.1 - C, Bb & Eb
The Digital Standards Songbook - individual songs with lyrics, plus C, Bb, Eb, High Voice & Low Voice
The Digital Real Book (650 songs from all our books)

THE DIGITAL SONGBOOK SERIES
The Kenny Barron Songbook
The Carla Bley Songbook
The Tom Harrell Songbook
The Oscar Hernandez Songbook
The Alan Pasqua Songbook
The Horace Silver Songbook
The Steve Swallow Songbook
The Ralph Towner Songbook
The Wayne Wallace Songbook
The Kenner Werner Songbook
The Randy Brecker Songbook
The Larry Dunlap Songbook
The Barry Finnerty Songbook
The Benny Golson Songbook
The Steve Khan Songbook
The Doug Morton Songbook
The Andy Narell Songbook
The Enrico Pieranunzi Songbook
The Dave Tull Songbook
The Denny Zeitlin Songbook

FOR STUDENT MUSICIANS
The Real Easy Book - Vol. 1 - C, Bb, Eb & Bass Clef
The Real Easy Book - Vol. 2 - C, Bb, Eb & Bass Clef
The Real Easy Book - Vol. 3 - C, Bb, Eb & Bass Clef
The Latin Real Easy Book - C, Bb, Eb & Bass Clef
Drum Supplement for Real Easy Book - Vol. 1
The Blues Scales - C, Bb, Eb, Bass Clef & Guitar
Rhythm First! - C, Bb, Eb & Bass Clef - by Tom Kamp
Guitarist's Introduction to Jazz - by Randy Vincent
Walking Bassics - by Ed Fuqua
Foundation Exercises for Bass - by Chuck Sher

CDs
Poetry+Jazz: A Magical Marriage - by Chuck Sher
Play-Along CDs for The New Real Book - Vol.1
The Latin Real Book Sampler CD

continued on next page

SHER MUSIC CO. JAZZ METHOD BOOKS
available in both print & digital forms

GUITAR
Jazz Guitar Voicings: The Drop 2 Book
  - Randy Vincent
Three-Note Voicings and Beyond - Randy Vincent
Line Games - Randy Vincent
Jazz Guitar Soloing: The Cellular Approach
  - Randy Vincent
The Guitarist's Introduction to Jazz - Randy Vincent
Contemporary Latin Jazz Guitar - Neff Irizarry

PIANO
The Jazz Piano Book - Mark Levine
Jazz Piano Masterclass: The Drop 2 Book - M. Levine
How To Voice Standards at the Piano - Mark Levine
An Approach to Comping - Vol. 1 - Jeb Patton
An Approach to Comping - Vol. 2 - Jeb Patton
Introduction to Jazz Piano: A Deep Dive - Jeb Patton
Playing for Singers - Mike Greensill
Wisdom of the Hand - Marius Nordal
The Jazz Solos of Chick Corea - Peter Sprague

SAXOPHONE
The Practice Notebooks of Michael Brecker
The Jazz Saxophone Book - Tim Armacost

VOiCE
The Digital Standards Songbook - individual songs with lyrics, plus C, Bb, Eb, High Voice & Low Voice
The Jazz Singer's Guidebook - David Berkman

DRUMS
Syncopation Companion - Bryan Bowman
Inner Drumming - George Marsh
Drum Supplement for Real Easy Book Vol.1 - Alan Hall
Afro-Caribbean Grooves for Drumset - JPhi Fanfant

TRUMPET
New Orleans Trumpet - Jim Thornton
Modern Etudes for Solo Trumpet - Cameron Pearce

BASS
The Improvisor's Bass Method - Chuck Sher
Concepts for Bass Soloing - Marc Johnson & C. Sher
Walking Bassics - Ed Fuqua
Foundation Exercises for Bass - Chuck Sher

JAZZ THEORY AND HARMONY
The Jazz Theory Book - Mark Levine
The Jazz Harmony Book - David Berkman
Forward Motion - Hal Galper
Metaphors for the Musician - Randy Halberstadt
Minor is Major! - Dan Greenblatt
Rhythm Changes Guide - Lukas Gabric
Jazz Scores and Analysis - Vol.1 - Richard Lawn
Jazz Scores and Analysis - Vol. 2 - Richard Lawn
The Blues Scales - C, Bb, Eb, Bass Clef & Guitar
    - Dan Greenblatt

PRACTICE GUIDES
The Practice Notebooks of Michael Brecker
Jazz Musician's Guide to Creative Practicing
    - David Berkman
The Serious Jazz Practice Book - Barry Finnerty
The Serious Jazz Book II - Barry Finnerty
Building Solo Lines from Cells - Randy Vincent

EAR TRAINING
The Real Easy Ear Training Book - Roberta Radley
Reading, Writing and Rhythmetic - Roberta Radley

RHYTHM SECTION GUIDES
Essential Grooves - Moretti, Stagnaro & Nicholl
Inside the Brazilian Rhythm Section - Nelson Faria
    & Cliff Korman
The Salsa Guidebook - Rebeca Mauleón
Decoding Afro-Cuban Jazz - Mauleón & Valdes

BILINGUAL OR LIBROS EN ESPANOL
101 Montunos - Rebeca Mauleón
Muy Caliente! - Afro-Cuban Book & Play-Along
El Libro del Jazz Piano - Mark Levine
The Latin Real Book - C, Bb and Eb

MISCELLANEOUS
Method for Chromatic Harmonica - Max de Aloe
Jazz Songs for the Student Violinist
    - Kevin Mitchell & Joanne Keefe

Sign up for our monthly discount newsletter by writing shermuse@sonic.net